FAMILY Life ISSUES

Growing as a Blended Family

By Joseph Barbour
and Donna Steiner

D1403245

CPH.
SAINT LOUIS

Editor: Rodney L. Rathmann
Editoral Assistant: Phoebe W. Wellman

Write to Library for the Blind, 1333 S. Kirkwood Road, St. Louis, MO 63122-7295 to obtain *Growing as a Blended Family* in braille and in large print for the visually impaired. Allow 12 weeks for processing. Call for an updated list.

Copyright © 1994 Concordia Publishing House
3558 S. Jefferson Avenue, St. Louis, MO 63118-3968
Manufactured in the United States of America

2 3 4 5 6 7 8 9 10   03 02 01 00

Contents

Introduction

▲ How to Use This Course

This course has been especially prepared for use in small group settings. It may, however, also be used as a self-study or in a traditional Sunday morning Bible class.

▲ Planning for a Small Group Study

1. *Select a leader* for the course or a leader for the day. It will be the leader's responsibility to secure needed materials, to keep the discussion moving, and to help involve everyone.

2. *Emphasize sharing.* Your class will work best if the participants feel comfortable with one another and if all feel that their contributions to the class discussion are important and useful. Take the necessary time at the beginning of the course to get to know one another. You might share names, occupations, hobbies, etc. Share what you expect to gain from this course. Invite participants to bring photos of their families to the first session to pass around as they introduce themselves and tell about the individual members of their families. Be open and accepting. Don't force anyone to speak. The course will be most helpful if participants willingly share deep feelings, problems, doubts, fears, and joys. That will require building an atmosphere of openness, trust, and caring among one another. Take time to build relationships among participants. That time will not be wasted.

3. *Help participants apply* the concepts included in each session. After each week's study, there is a suggested activity. An old Chinese proverb summarizes the "why?" of the activity:

I hear and I forget;
I see and I remember;

I do and I understand.

The activity is to help participants do and thus understand. Encourage everyone to take time to do it.

4. Encourage participants to invite their friends—including their unchurched friends—to be a part of this study.

▲ As You Plan to Lead the Group

1. Read this guide in its entirety before you lead the first session.

2. Use the Leader Notes found in the back of this guide.

3. Pray each day for those who join the group.

4. As you prepare for each session, study the Bible texts thoroughly. Work through the exercises for yourself. Depend on the Holy Spirit. Expect His presence; He will guide you and cause you to grow. God will not let His Word return empty (Isaiah 55:11) as you study it both individually and with the others in the group.

5. Do not expect the Spirit to do your work for you. Start early. Prepare well. As time permits, do additional reading about the topic.

6. Begin and end with prayer.

7. Begin and end on time. Punctuality is a courtesy to everyone and can be a factor that will encourage discussion.

8. Find ways to keep the session informal: meet in casual surroundings. Arrange seating so participants can face one another. Ask volunteers to provide refreshments.

9. Keep the class moving. Limit your discussion to questions of interest to the participants. Be selective. You don't need to cover every question and every Bible verse.

10. Build one another up through your fellowship and study. You have your needs; other group members have theirs. Together you have a lot to gain.

11. Be sensitive to any participants who may have needs related to the specific problems discussed in this course, especially anyone who may need Christian counseling and professional help.

12. Be a "gatekeeper." That means you may need to shut the gate on one person while you open it for someone else. Involve everyone, especially those who hesitate to speak.

▲ If You Are Using This Study on Your Own

1. Each time you sit down to study a session, ask the Holy Spirit for guidance and counsel. Expect Him to work through His Word to encourage, motivate, and empower you to grow in your faith.

2. Study the Bible texts, printed in the course, with special care. God works through His Word. In it you will find power. Read each text slowly, several times.

3. Write answers in the spaces provided. Avoid the temptation just to "think" your responses. Writing will force you to be specific. It's in that specificity you are most likely to identify crucial issues for yourself. Check the Leader Notes in the back of this guide for information you may find helpful as you go along.

4. Pray as you work. Ask God to show you what He wants you to see about Him, about yourself, and about your family situation.

A Special Kind of Family

Opening Prayer

Heavenly Father, You have taught us to build our family foundations on Your Word. Help us to turn our eyes to You as we study the unique gifts of our blended families. Give us patience, understanding, and forgiveness as we build in Your name. Amen.

Focusing Our Attention

Blended families, or stepfamilies, form when two adults establish a household in which at least one of the adults has a child or children from a previous relationship.

Think about the blended family to which you belong or about a blended family with which you are acquainted. Choose an item from among the following and explain how this item reminds you of this family.

1. a sandwich
2. a tossed salad
3. scrambled eggs
4. leftovers
5. mixed nuts
6. chicken with baby potatoes
7. Thanksgiving dinner

Valuing Differences

The blended family is a unique kind of family. Past experiences and varied backgrounds offer the potential for a family life that is both enriching and challenging. Many blended families today face the task of building a blended family with high hopes but little or no preparation.

1. Name some factors that make blended families different from traditional families?

2. Of all the factors discussed, which do you think is the most difficult to accept?

3. What are some of the strengths of a blended family?

Beginning Again

When Mary's husband, Don, died in a car accident, she felt as though her life was over. Then she met John. Newly divorced and the father of two, John gave her reason to live again. Together they dreamed of picking up the pieces of their broken lives and starting over. Building their relationship around Christ, they trusted that His love and care and their love for one another would help them make it through the rough times.

The first year of marriage was more challenging for John and Mary than either had expected. Mary struggled with keeping up with her job, her new husband, and her children. Sometimes she felt indifferent towards John's children and she worried something was wrong. John wasn't sure where he fit into this new family. He missed daily contact with his children; sometimes he felt guilty. John and Mary had very different ways of doing things and argued about who was right. At times both of them wondered if they had moved into marriage too soon.

John and Mary struggled to build one family where previously there had been two. Things didn't go at all as they had expected. If you were to talk with either of them today, they would identify for you several myths about blending two families together.

Instant Love

John: I guess I expected it would be easy for us to join together to be a family—like the Brady Bunch. But there is no such thing as an instant family. Blending a family and developing loving and trusting relationships within it takes time, patience, and effort. Family building within a blended family is a gradual, long-term process. In an excellent book I read recently, entitled *How to Win as a Stepfamily,* authors Emily and John Visher estimate that an integrated blended family takes approximately 3–5 years depending on the ages of the children—the younger the children the quicker the process.

Blended Families Should Work Just like Nuclear Families

Mary: I had to come to grips with the fact that I live in a new family now. I love John very much; but the relationship John and I share differs from my life with my first husband. John and I each have children and his children only live with us part of the time. Both of us have had other spouses; John's ex-wife is still a part of our lives since his children live with her most of the time.

Stepparents Are Cruel and Insensitive

John: Maybe it comes from reading stories such as *David Copperfield* or *Cinderella*, but I think children and even adults sometimes expect stepparents to treat the children of their spouse as though they are an inconvenience—an unwanted intrusion into a marriage. I can honestly say I want nothing better than for Mary's children to accept and like me. Even if they don't ever come to love me as a parent, I would like them to come to regard me as a valued friend.

Our Children Will Feel as Happy about Remarrying as We Do

Mary: My children were excited when we were first married; they were getting a new father. John's children had mixed emotions. I can understand it better now. After all, they still had their mother. Though they were pleased to see their father happy, deep down they may blame me that their parents were not together, even though the divorce occurred before

▼

John and I met. Plus, I suppose our marriage destroys any hope they might have harbored for their parents to get back together again.

Confusion and Chaos Are a Sign of Doom

John: How I worried when for a while, we just couldn't seem to get it together. It was like trying to fix something without a manual, using the trial and error method. Mary and I spent many late nights talking about things, praying about problems and struggles, and planning our strategies. Sometimes when things seem to be the most harried, they suddenly settled down. When things are quiet because no one is talking, I begin to worry.

Mary: The family John and I are building seems to find itself constantly going in a new direction. At times it can be frustrating, but God has kept us close together through everything. Through the struggles we have grown to know each other better and more quickly than we would have had we married each other without children.

John: Each family member in the blending process should talk about his or her expectations of life in the new family and discuss them openly. At first sharing feelings may be difficult; but if it leads to honesty and the deepening of relationships, it will have been worth it.

1. How can believing the myths about blended families affect the family-building process?

2. How might the hidden agendas of spouses and children in a blended family hamper developing relationships?

3. Explain the role of communication in family building.

The Need to Say Good-bye

Part of forming a new family involves acknowledging and working through unresolved grief. Two people entering marriage for the first time usually have not experienced the major loss by death or divorce that members of a blended family have known. Consider Jan.

Jan was crying a lot and she didn't know why. She thought there must be something terribly wrong with her. She had been married to Gary for four months and had to move from another city with her nine-year-old son, Zach. During the past five years she had managed a small office and loved her job. Her grandparents helped baby-sit Zach. She missed the support from her church and the spiritual guidance of

▼

her pastor. Many important losses had gone unrecognized and Jan felt drained and unhappy.

Loss of dreams and expectations, loss of a specific role in the family, and loss of support from family and friends regularly take their toll on the blended family. But with God's help, as losses are identified, mourned, and let go of, the family can move forward to a higher level of awareness and satisfaction.

1. What are some losses your children or stepchildren experienced before joining your blended family?

2. Which has had the greatest impact on your family?

3. Take the loss you have identified in item 2 and put into words how you feel about that loss. Now remind yourself of God and His great love for you. He knows you better than anyone ever has known you or ever will. He loves you with an unchanging, totally reliable love of extreme proportions. He gave the life of His only Son to earn forgiveness of sins, the chance for a completely new beginning, and an eternal home in heaven for you. He desires your happiness and well-being. Ask Him to help you accept your feelings about the past.

God's Promises for Today

All families are loved by God. He taught us the value of diversity. God promises that by faith we are all His children. Although the world around us is constantly changing, we have a Savior who is the same yesterday, today, and forever.

When life in a blended family is not what is expected, members may feel disappointed, inadequate, or discouraged. God invites us to find in Him the strength and hope to move forward. Write a phrase or sentence applying each of the following verses from God's Word to your life today.

1. "So do not fear, for I am with you; do not be dismayed, for I am your God. I will strengthen you and help you; I will uphold you with My righteous right hand" (Isaiah 41:10).

2. "For as high as the heavens are above the earth, so great is His love for those who fear Him; as far as the east is from the west, so far has He removed our transgressions from us" (Psalm 103:11–12).

3. "Come to me, all you who are weary and burdened, and I will give you rest" (Matthew 11:28).

4. "Love covers over a multitude of sins" (1 Peter 4:8).

5. "God has said, 'Never will I leave you; never will I forsake you'" (Hebrews 13:5).

A Look Ahead

What ideas or strategies might a Christ-centered blended family find helpful in dealing with loss, myths, expectations, and the changing world around us? Check any of the following that will assist you, as with God's help, you build healthy family relationships.

_____ Hold family meetings in which everyone has a say (set the tone by beginning and ending the meeting with a prayer).

_____ Pray together with your spouse and/or children as you ride together in the car.

_____ Make family meals an occasion to celebrate each other and your life together.

▼

_____ Plan a family meal or project complete with a list of designated responsibilities, involving every member of the family.

_____ Arrange to date your spouse without children.

_____ Ask God, "Please change our family; begin by changing me."

_____ Hold regular family nights, set aside solely for the purposes of being together to play games or simply to talk—sharing hopes, feelings, joys, disappointments, or to make family plans.

_____ Worship together regularly as a family.

To Do at Home

Plan time this week to share information and feelings about losses in your blended family.

Discuss myths and expectations.

Listen intently to each other.

Remind one another of the Good News that we are forgiven through Christ's death and resurrection. Jesus remains our constant in the ever-changing world around us.

Talk with one another about the special strengths and gifts God has brought into your lives with the creation of your Christ-centered blended family.

Closing Prayer

Heavenly Father, give us the patience and wisdom to understand and value all people and all families. Help us to trust in You and the power of Your unchanging Word. Thank You for the many gifts You have given us, including the gift of our blended family. In Jesus' name we pray. Amen.

Forming New Relationships

2 ▼

Opening Prayer

Dear Lord, help us to feel Your presence as we move from being one family to forming another family from two. Help us to understand that it is within families that our emotions are most closely tied and that changing relationships is an emotional process. We pray this in the name of Your Son, who changed our relationship with You, making us Your children through faith in Him. Amen.

Focusing Our Attention

Life in a blended family provides opportunities for persons of various ages to enter into and establish relationships with one another. Unfortunately, at times, these new relationships can create individual and family stress. Read the following quotes about various aspects of relationships in a blended family. Then choose one quote and tell the groups whether or not you agree with it and why.

1. "Children benefit in blended families because they have more adults in their lives who love and care for them."

2. "You are a better stepparent if you yourself have a stepparent."

3. "Once you remarry, your old in-laws are no longer part of your family."

4. "I treat my grandchildren and my stepgrand-children exactly the same."

5. "Stepparents do well to avoid getting involved in the discipline of their spouses' children."

New Relationships for Everybody

When a man and a woman marry and begin to relate to one another as husband and wife, they also redesign relationships for other family members in every generation. Typically, the defining and redefining of relationships occurs over a period of years. During a divorce, the relationships are drastically changed. Following the divorce, the relationships move toward becoming more stabilized. As the new marriage approaches, all of the relationships are suddenly out of balance again and must be realigned.

It is probably easiest to think of these relationship changes in terms of roles and role changes. As one side of a relationship changes, the other side must inevitably change to accommodate it if the relationship is to survive. If one side or the other refuses to change, it brings the whole system to a halt.

For example, if the former spouse of the new wife refuses to recognize the role of the new husband as a parent, the children will be forced to choose one over the other, a difficult task since they need both. It also forces the wife to choose sides on parenting issues. Choosing sides is also difficult since the children must be able to relate to both their parents and their stepparents.

1. What consequences might result from a situation in which the grandparents refuse to acknowledge their son or daughter's new spouse in favor of the biological parent of their grandchildren?

2. What consequences might result when a biological parent continually displays open hostility toward the other biological parent and his or her family?

3. Why do children need relationships with stepparents, stepgrandparents, stepsiblings, and other steprelatives?

Blending the Old and the New

When role changes are being developed, it is necessary to think of loyalty ties. For children, being loyal to one biological parent sometimes means that they must betray the other. It is hard for them to understand that they can be loyal to their biological father and the stepfather as well. For children, it takes time to believe that changing is not betraying.

To the individuals trying to cope with the changes, worry and confusion are uppermost; loyalty takes a back seat to simply surviving. So much time is spent trying to keep from hurting anyone that the self gets lost. If the pressure to be loyal continues, or if family members feel hurt in any way, emotional distance is created. Perhaps the most common feeling among all three generations during the blending of a family is that of loneliness; being disconnected in the midst of all of these people. Hesitation to accept new

▼

roles for themselves or the new roles for others is often a form of self-protection, not irritation.

There is no manual for being a stepbrother or stepsister. There is no manual on how to relate to four sets of grandparents, nor is there a manual explaining what to buy the new stepgrandchildren versus the biological grandchildren for Christmas. Each new relationship must be worked out one at a time.

Two things will help blended families work out their relationships one at a time. These are:

First, place Christ at the very center of all of these relationships. He loves us and our families with the strongest possible love. He lived, died, and rose again for each of us. His presence in our blending families brings family members forgiveness and patience as roles stabilize.

Second, keep the marriage as the primary relationship. It is from the marital relationship that other family members take their cue. When the marriage is strong, there is a feeling of hope. This is similar to knowing that Christ is the center of all that we do; regardless of how we feel now, we have hope in Christ.

Consider the power of God's love as it is described for us in **1 Corinthians 13,** "Love is patient, love is kind. It does not envy, it does not boast, it is not proud. It is not rude, it is not self-seeking, it is not easily angered, it keeps no record of wrongs. Love does not delight in evil but rejoices with the truth. It always protects, always trusts, always hopes, always perseveres" (vv. 4–7).

The kind of love described above is God's love for us. On our own, humans are incapable of this kind of love. Nevertheless, as God's forgiveness for us in Christ changes us, His Holy Spirit moves us to act upon and show His love to others. Give one or two examples of God's love as it might be demonstrated in actions and attitudes between each of the following:

1. the spouses in the blended family

2. stepparents and children

3. stepsiblings

4. grandparents and the stepgrandparents of their grandchildren

5. spouses and in-laws from a previous marriage

Avoiding Obstacles to Successful Redesigning of Relationships

When families come together, it is typical that the larger home of the two is selected, the smaller one sold or the lease is allowed to expire. When there are children from both of the spouses, the bedrooms that are available are split so that the newcomers will feel at home. This splitting of personal space, though unavoidable, can cause resentment and anger.

When noncustodial children are involved, even though bedroom space is made available, there is still a sense of who is a native of the house, and who is the visitor. When it is possible, the best solution is to find a place to live that is new to everyone. This eliminates the visitor/native controversy and avoids splitting personal space.

Former spouses need to be aware of the events taking place in the lives of their children. Certainly a remarriage of the parent is an event. Asking for the former spouse's acceptance and their help in moving their children toward acceptance will ease the transition for the children. This also implies to the former spouse that he/she will remain an essential part of their children's lives.

Grandparents and stepgrandparents should be assured that visitation will continue. Solid direction as to your expectations will be greatly appreciated.

The following suggestions can be used as a guideline to facilitate the role changes as a blended family comes together:

1. Spend time in prayer asking for guidance. During this time you may feel overwhelmed and unsure of who you are and how you are supposed to relate.

2. Discuss and agree with your spouse what the expectations are to be within the family and between family members. This creates clear boundaries that makes it possible for family members to become closer.

3. Decide on a means of solving family squabbles. Stick with it.

4. Discuss openly the relationship family members want to have with each other. Discuss the relationship they want to have with the extended family members, such as grandparents, in-laws, cousins, and others.

5. Model that relationship building takes time and that some may have more difficulty than others. Agree that everyone in the family will treat one another with kindness and respect.

6. Develop a strong spiritual life that the family revolves around, rather than an angry center that everyone avoids.

Exercise

Share how you handled your first Christmas as a blended family. How did you deal with issues of family celebrations and gift-giving? What might you have done differently knowing what you know now.

To Do at Home

On a large piece of paper, list all family members in all generations, making sure to include every significant relationship. Draw two lines between family members who feel comfortable with each other and a broken line between family members who do not get along with each other. How many broken lines are there? What do these people need in order to be connected? How is the family diminished or helped by the distance between these members? Pray for an opportunity to reconnect the broken lines when possible.

Closing Prayer

Dear Father, You alone provide the means by which we find the strength to forgive and go on. Bring Your healing and growing presence into our new relationships. We pray this in Your Son's name. Amen.

3
The New Couple

Opening Prayer

Father in heaven, You taught us about relationships through Your Son's relationship with us. Teach us today how to be in a relationship with our spouse and children so that we may reside in peace with one another and with You. Be present in our relationships and grant that we may grow stronger as you strengthen our faith. We pray in Jesus' name. Amen.

Focusing Our Attention

Which of the following road signs best describes you and your spouse during the past week? Explain.

1. Merging Traffic
2. One Way
3. Construction Ahead
4. Stop
5. Reduce Speed
6. Yield
7. Children at Play

Staying Close

One of the toughest tasks facing the new marriage is getting time to develop closeness. From the first date, there are numerous responsibilities that cause interruptions and eat up the time and energy so desperately needed by the couple trying to figure out if they are compatible. And then comes marriage. Many newlyweds enjoy reflecting on their wedding ceremony—everything was beautiful ... so many friends present ... everyone seemed to have a good time—only to have their thoughts interrupted with, "When's breakfast? I'm starving," from one child and "There is no milk!" from another.

Children can be a tremendous drain on a married couple's time and energy—commodities that newlyweds need for themselves if their marriage is going to be filled with closeness. In a traditional family, the advent of children brings a closeness to the couple. In a blended family, the children are one of the primary reasons for marital conflict.

Guilt plays a key role in a parent's unwillingness to take the time necessary to develop closeness. As a husband and wife pull toward each other, their children may feel the couple is pulling away from them. This creates resentment that may not be understood but emerges as anger toward the spouse or the children.

As the new couple becomes closer, the children sense that their position with their parent is changing. They mistakenly believe that they must find new ways to interrupt the closeness or they might be replaced. Finding and maintaining a balance between reassuring your children and nurturing a closeness with your spouse can be difficult.

In all families, especially blended families, the children are an integral part of the marital relationship for only a portion of the total time of the marriage. If the marriage is built around children, then the marriage has no foundation when the children leave. Then too, when the marriage is built around the children, the children end up carrying the weight of the marriage. How *they* are doing at any one time will determine how the marriage is doing.

27
▼

1. List five ways that your children interrupt or prevent you from spending time with your spouse.

2. Think of a situation in which unnecessary guilt regarding the children prevented you from feeling close to your spouse.

3. Fortunately, God helps us put family relationships into their proper focus. In His Word God refers to marriage as a sacred institution from which children and in-laws emerge. What words of God describing the first man and wife—Adam and Eve—help us to identify the husband and the wife as the primary relationship in a marriage?

"For this reason a man will leave his father and mother and be united to his wife, and they will become one flesh" (Genesis 2:24).

4. What can we learn from the following verses about the relationship between husbands and their wives? between Christ and those who love and trust in Him?

"Wives, submit to your husbands as to the Lord. For the husband is the head of the wife as Christ is the head of the church, His body, of which He is the Savior. Now as the church submits to Christ, so also wives should submit to their husbands in everything. Husbands, love your wives, just as Christ loved the

▼

church and gave Himself up for her to make her holy, cleansing her by the washing with water through the Word, and to present her to Himself as a radiant church, without stain or wrinkle or any other blemish, but holy and blameless. In this same way, husbands ought to love their wives as their own bodies. He who loves his wife loves himself. After all, no one ever hated his own body, but he feeds and cares for it, just as Christ does the church—for we are members of His body" (Ephesians 5:22–31).

Conflict in the Blended Family

As two families come together to form one, conflict and turmoil between family members is both inevitable and necessary. However, new spouses sometimes identify turmoil as being a sign that the marriage is a mistake. Fear creeps in between the husband and the wife, creating distance. Suddenly, spouses find themselves saying things like, "Perhaps something is wrong since we are not as happy as we are supposed to be."

It is helpful to know that turmoil and conflict are normal. Inevitable conflicts will emerge in schedules, wants, needs, plans, beliefs, etc. when two families are blended. People in conflict can react in a number of ways—withdrawing, insisting on winning, yielding, compromising, or working to resolve the conflict.

Read each of the following situations:

• At the first hint of a disagreement Maria changes the subject, ignores the other person, leaves the room or the house, or goes to sleep.

• In the heat of conflict, Ross loses sight of people, relationships, even issues, as he presses on to victory.

• "I give up. We'll do it your way," Jacob sighed. He still believed that he had the better solution for the Saturday schedule problem, but gave in rather than spending hours arguing with Susan.

1. What might be the result of Maria's reaction?

Ross' reaction?

Jacob's reaction?

2. How might have Maria, Ross, and Jacob dealt more appropriately with the conflict?

Now read the following situation:

Jim and Betty disagreed on an appropriate curfew for their teenage sons. Betty's 16-year-old son had been allowed to stay out until 1:00 a.m., while Jim's 17-year-old son had to be in by midnight. The newly married couple agreed that they had a difference of opinion, but committed themselves to resolve their disagreement without involving the two boys. After discussing the pros and cons and exploring several alternatives, Jim and Betty agreed that both boys needed a 12:30 curfew.

3. What might be the result of Jim and Betty's reaction to the conflict?

4. What are some benefits to compromise?

5. What are the benefits of committing yourself to resolving conflicts?

6. Write a phrase or sentence to apply each of the following Bible verses to conflict resolution and building healthy relationships in blended families.

"For He Himself is our peace, who has made the two one and has destroyed the barrier, the dividing wall of hostility" (Ephesians 2:14).

"If You, O LORD, kept a record of sins, O Lord, who could stand? But with You there is forgiveness; therefore You are feared" (Psalm 130:3–4).

▼

"Therefore, if anyone is in Christ, he is a new creation; the old has gone, the new has come!" (2 Corinthians 5:17).

"I can do everything through Him who gives me strength" (Philippians 4:13).

"Your Word is a lamp to my feet and a light for my path" (Psalm 119:105).

Working It Through

Consider the following suggestions to help you grow closer to your spouse. Place an × before those things you are already doing. Place a + before those ideas you plan to do.

_____ 1. Spend time discussing your fears with your heavenly Father. Pray together, meet together for devotions with your spouse and the rest of your family.

_____ 2. When you feel angry, ask yourself what you fear. Then share that fear with your spouse. This prevents angry, blaming remarks that create distance.

_____ 3. Set limits with all of the children in the household so that you and your spouse have time to spend together each day or at least several times a week.

_____ 4. While openly supporting your spouse with genuine compliments, demonstrate that you trust your spouse by your honesty.

_____ 5. Find extended periods of time together without the children.

_____ 6. Keep the romantic flame burning in your marriage. Avoid old patterns of being together. Create new patterns by going to new places and trying new events together.

_____ 7. Understand that the time you spend away gives the siblings an opportunity to develop their own relationships.

_____ 8. Consciously guard your marriage relationship from intrusion by the children, grandparents, and ex-spouses.

_____ 9. See your spouse as Christ does, clean and perfect and forgiven.

To Do at Home

Write your spouse a love letter. Tell your spouse which of his or her qualities you thank God for when you pray.

Closing Prayer

Lord, You have placed the husband and wife relationship at the center of all family relationships. Help us feel Your presence in the heart of our marriage relationships. We pray in Jesus' name. Amen.

4 ▼ The Parenting Partnership

Opening Prayer

Father of all families, be present in our family life. Teach us to rely upon each other as only family members can. But teach us a greater reliance upon You. Forgive us for Jesus' sake for the times we have been wrong, and give us patience and perseverance as we struggle to find our place in the family You have given us. In Jesus' Name we pray. Amen

Focusing Our Attention

Family life becomes pleasant and fulfilling when family members relate to one another and function as a team. Think of your family as a baseball team. Assign team-member designations to each member of your family. Use these designations to introduce your children to the others in the group. Explain why you identified each child as you did.

Co-captains _____ _____
(husband)   (wife)

Pitcher _____ First Base_____

Catcher_____ Second Base_____

Base-runner _____ Third Base _____

Short Stop _____ Outfield_____

Becoming a Parent to Your Spouse's Children

After creating a strong husband-wife bond, the second most important and usually the most difficult part of blending a family is in developing a parenting partnership. When both husband and wife bring children into a marriage, the difficulties increase.

When divorce by one or both spouses precedes the new blended family, things become complicated even further. Divorce changes the way families view themselves and their relationship to God. Frequently, those living in the wake of a divorce have learned that the world can be an unsafe place and may feel that God is far away. Things that only seem to happen to others, suddenly happen to them. Unwanted change for the children keeps popping up after divorce. Often remarriage quickly follows divorce in the anxious attempt to find stability once again.

Raising children is an awesome task when both parents are available. But single parents often have no one with whom they can discuss important parenting decisions. Even day-to-day decisions overwhelm many single parents. New partners look forward to having someone with whom to share parenting decisions and responsibilities. Single parents often experience a feeling of relief when they remarry at the comforting anticipation that now there will be someone to help them.

1. List some difficulties you would expect or did expect at the thought of being a stepparent or of sharing the parenting of your children with someone not your children's biological parent.

2. Consider the following verses from God's Word. Then, reflecting upon each, list some benefits that can result from stepparenting.

a. "Carry each other's burdens, and in this way you will fulfill the law of Christ. Therefore, as we have opportunity, let us do good to all people, especially to those who belong to the family of believers" (Galatians 6:2, 10).

b. "Train a child in the way he should go, and when he is old he will not turn from it" (Proverbs 22:6).

c. "All your sons will be taught by the LORD, and great will be your children's peace" (Isaiah 54:13).

d. "Posterity will serve Him; future generations will be told about the Lord. They will proclaim His righteousness to a people yet unborn—for He has done it" (Psalm 22:30–31).

e. "Dear friends, let us love one another, for love comes from God. Everyone who loves has been born of God and knows God. Whoever does not love does not know God, because God is love" (1 John 4:7–8).

Back to the Future

When the first child was born, the biological parents typically worked out together how the parenting was to be done. Since they had to start from scratch, they relied on the model of parenting they experienced while they were growing up. To develop their own model, they had to figure out which parts of the way in which they were parented they wanted to keep. When the father's model conflicted with the mother's model, they had to negotiate with each other which model or parts of each model they were going to use.

These negotiations may have taken the form of talking, yelling, fighting, being stubborn, or any form of problem solving that was successful in the past. Resolving struggles of this type can be difficult, because to give in to the spouse's view can be seen as a betrayal of one's own upbringing.

Usually, however, after much time and expended energy, a new, common model for parenting is born. Generally, as the child ages and becomes more complex, so does the new parenting model.

To avoid additional change and conflict, it is usually assumed by both partners of a new marriage in which spouses have been married before that the other will slip into the slot created in the last marriage. As each waits for the other to change to the "preferred" parenting style, concern begins to heighten. This concern is not unlike two boxers in the ring who circle at the beginning of a fight waiting to see what the other is going to do.

Most likely, one of the driving forces behind the marriage itself was to slow down change and to stabilize the living environment for the children. Since there may be two sets of parenting models, new negotiations soon have to begin. If the newly married couple waits too long to start negotiations, even for the sake of a sense of stability, the family will remain two families. Each parent will remain loyal to his or her parenting style, and each child will be loyal to only one parent.

When a blended family chooses to remain two parallel families in the same house, it becomes difficult for the non-biological parent to correct a child. Often unconsciously, the biological parent will seek to protect his or her child from the non-biological parent.

Remaining two parallel families within a marriage gives the children permission to hear only one parent. It creates disappointment and resentment from the other spouse creating a distance between the two.

1. List five major ways that your parenting style differs from that of your spouse.

a. _____

b. _____

c. _____

d. _____

▼

e. _____

2. What impact have these differences had on the children?

3. What impact has this had on your marriage?

Working as a Team

In order for children to feel safe, their parents must work together as partners. The differing ideas about children that spouses bring into second marriages may ultimately serve to make the parenting partnership stronger and more effective. These differences can become a tremendous source of new ideas and a means to get unstuck from former parenting techniques that were not working.

By God's grace, as the primary relationship—the marriage—strengthens, so does the ability to include ideas from both parents to create a newer, better, style of parenting. From this the children learn how to negotiate in a loving environment so that everyone wins.

Relationship-building between stepparents and children usually takes time. As a general rule, the more a parent pushes children to develop a positive relationship with the new spouse, the longer it will take to happen. Sometimes it takes up to five years to normalize the relationships in a blended family. The most effective way for these relationships to happen is to relax and stay out of the way.

A major difference for children between a blended family and a traditional family is that the children in the blended family may have as many as four parents. It is natural that a child's loyalty will be to both biological parents. So when children feel that a new spouse wants to replace their noncustodial parent, they rebel, plot, and yell that it will never happen. And of course, it doesn't. Initially allowing the new parent to act as a friend instead of a parent can remove some of the tension from both.

Therefore, it may be helpful at first for the biological parent to assume the major responsibility for their child. Gradually this responsibility can be shifted to become a shared effort.

In addition, at the beginning of a new marriage, it usually helps to openly define for the children the difference between the spouse of a parent and a father or mother. If the new spouse is willing to encourage contact with the biological parent, much of the rebellion against the marriage will disappear.

Often in blended family situations, children fantasize about life with their noncustodial parent. "If only Dad were here, I wouldn't have to experience this." Keeping as many family members as possible freely in touch with each other speeds up the process of figuring out who belongs where in the family. It also reduces fear from the children that someone will somehow be replaced or not allowed to be in their lives.

In whatever type or condition of family situation we find ourselves, we can take comfort in the relationship God has established with us through His Son, Jesus Christ. He will help us find our way as we meet and adapt to change. His power and creative energy is at our disposal because by faith He has already made us into a special type of family—one in which He is the Father and we are His children.

John's first epistle records, "How great is the love the Father has lavished on us, that we should be called the children of God! And that is what we are!" (1 John 3:1). God has adopted us into His family through faith in Jesus who came to live, die, and rise to save us from our sin and from all that would jeop-

▼

ardize our forever-relationship with Him. In a very real way God has adopted us into His family as "children born not of natural descent, nor of human decision or a husband's will, but born of God" (John 1:13).

For Discussion

1. Tell why you agree or disagree with the statement, "God has no stepchildren."

2. Consider the following situation as it occurred within a month after Bob's marriage. If you were Bob how would you respond?

As Bob watched, his 10-year-old stepdaughter Heather walked over to the refrigerator, opened the door, stood forever, and finally removed a piece of that night's dessert. Bob's anger rose as he realized that dinner would be in less than an hour. "Why does her mom let her do that?" he wondered.

Help for Successful Parenting

The following are some suggestions for solving problems that will help you move toward parenting as a team:

1. Pray that God will guide your path as you begin your journey together.

2. Answer these questions before you begin: What does God want me to do in this situation? How can everyone win?

3. Set aside a time that will be free of children's interruptions.

4. Leave all excess emotional baggage outside of the discussions. This is a conversation between you and your spouse. Questions such as "What will my parents think?" or "What will my ex-spouse think?" should be kept outside.

5. Ask your spouse what it is that you do that creates an obstacle between your child and their parenting.

6. Decide what the issue is by each defining it. Take only one defined issue at a time. Share what you like about the way your spouse is handling the issue. Share what you do not like. Remember that both of you are doing the same thing—endeavoring to be the best parent possible for the children and the family.

To Try at Home

Choose one issue upon which you and your spouse disagree. Place an empty chair between you to represent Christ. Use the guidelines given above and resolve that issue. If you feel you are becoming more distant than close, take a break and try it again in five minutes.

Closing Prayer

Our Father, help us to look to You for direction and guidance for all of our decisions. Especially Father, help us to work as a team in such a way that the love You have for each of us in Christ Jesus will be reflected in all of our thoughts, words, and actions. We pray in Jesus' name. Amen.

Helping Your Child Adjust

5

Opening Prayer

Dear heavenly Father, You love and nurture us with perfect guidance, wisdom, and love. We look to You as our example for parenting. As Your Holy Spirit works in us through Your Word, give us the patience, insight, and strength to support and nurture our children in a way pleasing to You. In Jesus' name we pray. Amen.

Focusing Our Attention

Facing the possibility of marrying a man with two children, Abby contemplated married life and the thought of stepparenting. Suddenly, she was flooded with memories. Abby's mother and Bill had been married for several months when Bill decided to talk openly with her about their relationship. "Abby, I want you to know that I'm not trying to take your father's place. Still, I want you, your mother, and me to be a family."

Abby smiled remembering how hard and consistently Bill worked to make them a happy, secure family. Smiling, Abby looked at Bill and said, "You don't have to be a dad. You can be my 'special kind of' parent."

Think about the type of memories you would like your stepchildren to have. Which of the following memories would you most like your stepchildren to have of you?

_____1. Your support for them in their interests.

_____2. Never giving up on trying to build a good relationship, despite resistance.

_____3. Your continual efforts to make things fun.

_____4. Your willingness always to be there to talk with them.

_____5. Your encouragement of them always to do their best.

The Gift of Empathy

Although under any circumstances parenting can be challenging, stepparenting carries with it a double-challenge. Most stepparents feel at least some degree of apprehension about their role in rearing another's children. But with the Lord's help, as time passes, trust can develop and new bonds can be formed and strengthened between stepparents and children.

Effective parenting and stepparenting is usually done with empathy—the ability to look at life from the other person's point of view. As you think about yourself as a parent or stepparent ask yourself: Can I enter my stepson's world of feeling and experience? Can I feel my stepdaughter's loyalty conflict? Can I sense their sadness, loss, and indifference? In this session we will explore stepparenting by taking a look at the characteristics generally associated with three developmental stages—young children, ages 6–12, and teen years. Understanding the stepchild's needs and behaviors can help a stepparent empathize with him or her and the feelings he or she may be experiencing.

Young Children

Because young children attach themselves to marriage and parental stability, they may strongly oppose divorce and remarriage. Most children fantasize about their biological parents reuniting and their stepparent leaving. Then, too, the loss of familiar schedules and surroundings can be upsetting. Sometimes young children will cry and only reluctantly accompany the noncustodial parent to his or her household.

Young children react strongly to the feelings and behaviors of the adults around them. They will be looking to see if the mom or dad with whom they live is happy and how well she or he is handling a new situation. The more cooperation among the adults, the sooner the young child will adjust to the changes in his or her world.

Young children's understanding of words and language is emerging. Adults interacting with them sometimes struggle to communicate in a language they can understand. The younger the child, usually, the quicker the adjustment to blended-family life.

Ages 6–12

Eight-year-old Johnny misses his friends from the old neighborhood. His sister Kelly will have her seventh birthday tomorrow. When Mom asked her what she wanted for her birthday, Kelly hesitated a minute. Then, casting her stepfather, Mitch, an apologetic glance, Kelly said, "I want you and Daddy to get married to each other again."

"Honey," her mom replied, "You know that can't happen. What else do you want?"

This time her reply was quick and cheerful, "To go camping with you and Mitch. Will you take me?"

Kelly and Johnny are displaying some pretty typical behavior of this developmental stage. Their behavior can become difficult to deal with as they struggle with their feelings and the changing world around them. Children at this age need special reassurances that the divorce was not their fault. They need to be

45
▼

reminded that Jesus' love and the love of their parents for them are constants on which they can depend. Children do adapt to losses, but their adjustment depends on how well they are helped through the process. Give them as many choices as possible during this time and pray for understanding and healing.

After a family discussion, Johnny's mom found out he was frustrated over the lack of involvement in important family decisions. Kelly was able to talk about her secret wish for her parents to be together again. Through listening, empathizing, and the work of the Holy Spirit, the family was able to reconnect and discuss realities and possibilities.

Teenager

"Two parents are too many! I don't need still another adult telling me what to do."

Sixteen-year-old Sarah had been doing all the cooking for her father, and then in walked her new stepmother to rearrange the kitchen and make it hers. Fifteen-year-old Brett had taken pride in mowing the yard and being the man of the house, until his stepfather took over.

In most families, adolescence is viewed as a stage of crisis. The teenager's normal behavior—mood swings, rebellion, brooding, disobedience—can be maddening. Family clashes are common as they struggle toward independence. Teenagers are often reluctant to put forth the effort to become part of the new blended family. Family bonding is usually hampered when a teen's parents marry because family building is most difficult when the teenager's natural inclination is more toward independence.

Chaos and struggles that accompany teen years are normal and inevitable. They need not be signs of failure. Resolving crisis is the first step toward building unity and a sense of family.

Answer each of the following according to the age level of the child(ren) in your life.

1. What role do you play or hope to play in the life of your child or the child of your spouse?

2. What advantages may result from choosing your role rather than slipping into it?

3. Can you identify the child's most important need?

4. Share with the group blessings God has bestowed on your blended family with children from this age group.

God's Help for Family Building

God cares about people and families. He sent Jesus to earth to live a perfect life and to die a horrible death in order to bring us forgiveness, peace, and a new and eternal life in Him. As His Word touches our lives, His Holy Spirit guides and directs, motivates, and empowers us for the challenges we face.

1. Apply the following words from Holy Scripture to yourself as you attempt to understand and relate positively and effectively to your stepchild(ren).

a. Delight yourself in the LORD and He will give you the desires of your heart. Commit your way to the LORD; trust in Him and He will do this: He will make your righteousness shine like the dawn, the justice of your cause like the noonday sun (Psalm 37:4–5).

b. "If any of you lack wisdom, he should ask God, who gives generously to all without finding fault, and it will be given to him" (James 1:5).

c. "Confess your sins to each other and pray for each other so that you may be healed" (James 5:16).

d. "Where two or three come together in My name, there am I with them" (Matthew 18:20).

2. **Galatians 5:22** lists the results of the Holy Spirit working in the life of a Christian. Circle one or two of these that would be especially helpful for you in your family life right now.

"But the fruit of the Spirit is love, joy, peace, patience, kindness, goodness, faithfulness, gentleness and self-control."

To Try at Home

Complete the following:

As I review my journey to assist my children and stepchildren's adjustment process in our blended family:

Here's what I do that's effective.

Here's something I do that I would like to change.

With the help of the Holy Spirit and God's Word, here is my plan for change.

Closing Prayer

Dear Father in heaven, we thank and praise You for the gift of children. Give us the wisdom, patience, and understanding to know Your will. Help us rededicate our parenting and family life to Your glory. In Jesus' name we pray. Amen.

The Journey Forward

Opening Prayer

Heavenly Father, today we reflect on the blended-family Bible study and realize the complexities and challenges that face our special families. Forgive our past mistakes and heal us for Jesus' sake. Give us forgiving hearts as we relate to one another. Help turn our eyes to You today as we study Your Word, contemplating our journey forward. In Jesus' name we pray. Amen.

Focusing Our Attention

Choose one or more of the following statements. Share with a partner how that statement applies to family life.

1. Love is an emotion, but it is also a decision.

2. Following the path of least resistance is what makes rivers crooked.

3. While some pursue happiness, others create it.

4. A piece of iron worth $5.00 is the raw material from which $500,000 worth of watches can be made.

5. The archer hits the target, partly by pulling and partly by letting go.

Coming Together

Jamie stuck out his lower lip and complained,

"But we always have turkey on Sundays." Suddenly Kathy realized that the "we" Jamie was referring to was their blended family. They were beginning to establish their own traditions; the blending process had begun. Looking back Kathy wasn't sure how or when it started.

Helping new spouses and children develop a sense of "us" or "our family" seldom happens without a struggle. In order for relationships to develop and grow, issues must be shared honestly and openly in order that they might be resolved. Then, by God's grace, step-by-step, the individuals who have found themselves thrust together in a new household configuration gradually begin to see themselves as part of a new association—a family.

Jesus lived, died, and rose in order to provide us with a new and eternal life. His Holy Spirit makes those who love and trust in Him into new people, capable of thinking, speaking, and approaching things in new ways. His love and forgiveness form a unifying force that joins people to Him and to one another in the closest and most enduring of relationships.

1. Apply each of the following verses to your role in family-building.

a. "By the grace God has given me, I laid a foundation . . . but each should be careful how he builds. For no one can lay any foundation other than the one already laid, which is Christ Jesus" (1 Corinthians 3:10–11).

b. "Finally, brothers, whatever is true, whatever is noble, whatever is right, whatever is pure, whatever is lovely, whatever is admirable—if anything is excellent or praise-worthy—think about such things" (Philippians 4:8).

c. "In everything, do to others what you would have them do to you" (Matthew 7:12).

d. "We know that in all things God works for the good of those who love Him, who have been called according to His purpose." (Romans 8:28).

e. "He said to me, 'My grace is sufficient for you, for My power is made perfect in weakness'" (2 Corinthians 12:9).

f. "For nothing is impossible with God" (Luke 1:37).

2. What examples, however slight, can you cite to indicate that your blended family is beginning to come together?

Acceptance and Appreciation

Just as newlyweds learn to accept each other—blemishes and shortcomings included—stepparents learn to accept stepchildren for their own unique selves. As family building continues, each person claims his or her place. When individuals within blended families move toward acceptance of what can and cannot be, individual differences can become appreciated as rich, diverse perspectives.

Acceptance can lead to trust. Trust and respect can often, over time, become love through the power of the Holy Spirit.

1. Paul encourages believers, "Accept one another, then, just as Christ accepted you, in order to bring praise to God" (Romans 15:7). After reading the following passages, comment on the extent of God's acceptance of us. What is involved in similarly accepting others? "But God demonstrates His own love for

us in this: While we were still sinners, Christ died for us. . . . For if, when we were God's enemies, we were reconciled to Him through the death of His Son, how much more, having been reconciled, shall we be saved through His life!" (Romans 5:8, 10).

2. Consider the following verse.

"Dear children, let us not love with words or tongue but with actions and in truth. This then is how we know that we belong to the truth, and how we set our hearts at rest in His presence whenever our hearts condemn us. For God is greater than our hearts, and He knows everything" (1 John 3:18–20).

By the Spirit's power, how are God's people moved to respond to others even when they don't feel like loving?

3. What areas have you been able to accept and appreciate about your blended family? What areas continue to be a challenge?

Commitment

Commitment means making a choice to succeed and taking responsibility for working toward success. Committed families get out of the win-lose business. They no longer waste energy trying to place blame for the past. Just as God has committed Himself to us, persons in blending families can commit themselves to one another and to the new family. With the help of the Holy Spirit, they forgive and comfort one another with the forgiveness of Christ. Whenever progress is made in family building, however small, those involved can take heart and rejoice in what has been accomplished.

1. Comment on the following statement made by a newly married couple faced with the challenge of blending their family.

"Our commitment is first to God, then our marriage, then our family. God's enduring love continues to be our example for forgiveness, acceptance, and commitment."

2. Review the following list of ways families demonstrate acceptance, appreciation, and commitment. Extend the list, adding ideas and suggestions of your own.

a. Treat all family members respectfully.

b. Focus on God-given assets and strengths.

c. Get to know each other. Ask questions, inquire about each other's interests and preferences.

d. Give appreciative notes. Focus on small steps, not just final achievements.

e. Begin a "Child of the Week" program, highlighting the blessings, gifts, and achievements of each child. Some families begin a "Person of the Week" to include adult family members.

f. Laugh and have fun as a family.

g. _____

h. _____

i. _____

Traditions

One of the most important ways blended families build a solid identity is by establishing their own traditions. Celebrating holidays and special events year-after-year creates continuity and happy memories. Following is a list of ideas shared by other blended families. After considering the list, check one or more you would like to do in your family. Then involve your entire family in designing your own unique activities and events. Children love being part of the process of creating new traditions. Let the creative juices flow!

Share with the group traditions, celebrations, firsts, and ideas for creating unity that have worked in your blended families.

_____ a. Celebrate your anniversary as a blended family.

_____ b. Celebrate other "firsts": first move, first house, first picnic, first church service, first Christmas, etc.

_____ c. Plant a tree as a sign of growth together. Celebrate the beauty of God's creation. Nurture and feed the tree as you nurture and feed each other.

_____ d. Make a blended-family memory book charting the course. Include photographs, brochures from travel, art work, and anecdotes.

_____ e. Choose a family Bible verse, or have each member choose a verse and make a "family collection of verses."

_____ f. Create a blended family journal. Select a "family scribe" to write descriptions of events, group parties, individual performances, etc. Rotate the scribe weekly or monthly. Read the journal on a regular basis at family meetings.

_____ g. Holidays can be a source of stress for a blended family since children will often spend extended periods of time with the other parent. Choose a preholiday celebration that can be kept constant year after year. If family members are scattered on Christ-

▼

mas Day, establish a prayer time. First, write a family Christmas prayer together. Then establish a time, for example noon on Christmas Day for everyone to pray the designated prayer, wherever they may be at the time.

h._____

i. _____

j. _____

To Try at Home

Create a family "Coat of Arms." Placing Christ in the center, develop a blended-family crest. Have each family member contribute his or her ideas about what the crest should look like and contain. Each person can choose a specific symbol to represent themselves and all can be incorporated into the design. Some families may choose to have the final product professionally produced as a symbol of their unity.

Closing Prayer

Dear Father in heaven, You have blessed our blended families in many ways. Give us the patience to accept differences, the wisdom to listen and guide, the commitment to succeed—knowing that with You, nothing is impossible. Thank You for the opportunity to share with other blended families the strength of Your Word and the hope that is ours through Your Son, Jesus. In His name we pray. Amen.

Leader Notes

Session 1
A Special Kind of Family

▲ Focus

Welcome everyone. Give each participant a copy of the Study Guide. Encourage participants to write their names on the front covers. Ask that they take the booklets home between sessions and bring them back each time the group meets.

▲ Objectives

That by the power of the Holy Spirit working through God's Word the participants will
1. demonstrate an understanding of how blended families differ from other kinds of families;
2. affirm the forgiveness and healing God in Christ provides and the role He desires to have in family building;
3. gain insight into how to bridge two varied and unique family systems into one with Christ at the center;
4. distinguish between myths and realities of the blended family experience with God's Word as the foundation of truth.

▲ Opening Prayer

Comment that as with all families, blended families and the relationships within them need to be grown and nurtured.

Fortunately, we have a God who cares about everything, including our families. God loves all families and He will help us as we seek to grow closer to Him and to one another. Invite the group to join you in prayer as you read the words printed in the Study Guide.

▲ Focusing Our Attention

Define a blended family as a stepfamily, a family in which one or both of the spouses become a stepparent upon marriage. Use this activity to get the class off and running. If the class is large, divide it into groups of three or four. Ask participants to introduce themselves and describe a blended family according to the item of their choice. When it appears everyone has had a chance to share, reassemble the large group.

▲ Valuing Differences

Affirm the contents of the introductory paragraph; the process of blending families together often begins with high hopes but with little or no preparation. Continue with the section working through the questions either with the entire group or in small groups. Possible responses follow:

1. Traditional families are joined biologically; blended families are joined by biology and marriage. In traditional families the children have only one set of parents; children in blended families often have both parents and stepparents. Parents in traditional families begin their role at the birth or adoption of their children; parents in blended families begin parenting stepchildren when they marry the children's parents and they sometimes share parenting of the children with a parent and/or stepparent living in another household.

2. Answers will vary.

3. Blended families can find their strength in diversity of backgrounds and perspectives represented in them. Ideally, children in blended families have more adults who love and care about them than do children in traditional households.

▲ Beginning Again

Read or invite a volunteer to read aloud the introductory vignette aloud to the group. Comment that in this section we will explore several myths commonly associated with blended families. Invite volunteers to read the myths aloud to the whole group. Pause after each myth to comment or to listen to comments from the group. Discuss the questions with the whole group. Possible responses are as follows:

1. Adhering to the myths about blended families can keep individuals from forming family ties. It can also lead to frustration and disillusionment for parents, children, and stepparents.

2. Hidden agendas may adversely affect family building in a stepfamily situation. Although each individual involved may enter the blended family with his or her own set of expectations, relationships need to develop and grow individually, uniquely, and in their own time.

3. Open communication, in which feelings rather than value judgments are shared, can serve as a catalyst to growing relationships.

▲ The Need to Say Good-bye

Use the topic of communication to bridge this section with the preceding one. Say, **Communication is especially helpful when a new family must work through unresolved grief.** Read the introductory paragraph. Then have a volunteer read the vignette aloud. Read the paragraph following the vignette to the group.

Allow time for participants to work through the questions in this section individually. After several minutes, invite comments from the group, but force no one to share. Underscore the all-knowing, all-forgiving, all-powerful love of God for us through Christ Jesus our Lord. Then move on to the next section.

▲ God's Promises for Today

Read or paraphrase the introductory information. Then allow several minutes for participants to respond to the passages. After several minutes invite group members to share their thoughts or comments about each. Affirm the companionship and trusted friendship Jesus provides to all who love and believe in Him—including those struggling to build relationships.

▲ A Look Ahead

Encourage the members of the class to read and select ideas in this section that will help them as they work through the challenges and struggles with those closest to them and join together to build healthy family relationships. Conclude the activity commenting on the importance of inviting God to be the head and binding force in the family, of making marriage the primary family relationship, and of working to build effective communication within the family.

▲ To Do at Home

Encourage participants to set aside a time to do this activity during the coming week.

▲ Closing Prayer

Conclude the session by praying the prayer printed in the Study Guide or a prayer of your own.

Session 2

Forming New Relationships

Welcome everyone. Give each participant a copy of the Study Guide. Encourage participants to write their names on the front covers. Ask that they take the booklets home between sessions and bring them back each time the group meets.

▲ Objectives

That by the power of the Holy Spirit working through God's Word the participants will

1. identify why relationships can be difficult to change or develop;

2. recognize that relationships can be strengthened with the help of Christ, who desires to be at the center of all relationships;

3. affirm the virtue of patience when seeking to bring about change.

▲ Opening Prayer

Comment that blending a family is a process of developing new relationships and changing old ones. Say, **As we begin our study today, let's invite our Lord to join us and to give us the thoughts, insights, and understandings He would have us gain during this session.** Read the prayer printed in the Study Guide or expand on it to construct a prayer of your own.

▲ Focusing Our Attention

Read the introductory paragraph to the group and continue with the activity. If your group is large, ask participants to form smaller groups of three or four to do their sharing.

▲ New Relationships for Everybody

Ask participants to read this section aloud, taking turns, paragraph-by-paragraph. Insert comments between paragraphs if you choose. Continue with the questions, inviting participants to work through them in groups of three or four. After several minutes reassemble the whole group and review responses. Responses will vary. Encourage participants not to become bogged-down in the sharing of personal experiences. Rather urge them to focus on the stress tensions such as those described bring to the detriment of the whole family.

Comment that children benefit in proportion to the number of positive relationships they enjoy with those closely related to them—either biologically or through marriage.

▲ Blending the Old and the New

Ask participants to read to themselves the material leading up to the numbered items in this section. Move participants into small groups to share one or two examples of God's love demonstrated in actions and attitudes in each of the situations named. Then reassemble participants for large-group sharing. Invite volunteers to share one or two examples for each numbered item.

▲ Avoiding Obstacles to Successful Redesigning of Relationships

Have participants take turns reading the material in this section, paragraph-by-paragraph. Then ask participants to work with their partners or in small groups to review the numbered suggestions and to complete the next section.

▲ Exercise

After participants have shared with their partners or in small groups, reassemble the large group. Invite comments.

▲ To Do at Home

Encourage participants to complete this activity with their families during the week ahead.

▲ Closing Prayer

Select a volunteer to pray extemporaneously or use the prayer printed in the Study Guide.

Session 3

The New Couple

▲ Focus

Welcome everyone. Give each participant a copy of the Study Guide. Encourage participants to write their names on the front covers. Ask that they take the booklets home between sessions and bring them back each time the group meets.

▲ Objectives

That by the power of the Holy Spirit working through God's Word the participants will

1. identify Christ as the third partner in a healthy Christian marriage;

2. identify God's view of the relationship between husband and wife;

3. acknowledge that God often brings people closer together through times of conflict.

▲ Opening Prayer

Say, **God's design is for husband and wife to form the primary relationship in all families with Christ as the guiding and empowering foundation for the relationship.** Invite everyone to pray in unison the prayer printed in the Study Guide.

▲ Focusing Our Attention

Invite participants to assemble in pairs or in groups of

three or four to share the road sign that best describes the relationship between them and their spouses during the previous week. Spouses may or may not be in the same small group. Reassemble everyone and continue with the next section.

▲ Staying Close

Ask volunteers to read the paragraphs in this section. Allow several minutes for participants to respond to the first two items privately.

Continue with item 3. Affirm God's "one flesh union" as the foundational relationship for all other relationships in the family.

Invite responses to the questions included in item 4. Affirm responses that focus on the love and submission God would have married persons demonstrate toward one another in their special "one flesh" relationship. Christ loves His church (all persons of all time and all places who believe in Him) in the same way He would have husbands love their wives. Christ's love includes living, giving, and dying for the benefit of those He desires as His own.

▲ Conflict in the Blended Family

Invite a volunteer to read aloud the opening paragraphs. Then have participants read silently the situations. Ask, **How did each of the individuals react to conflict?** Maria withdrew from the conflict, Ross insisted on winning the conflict, and Jacob yielded to the conflict.

1. Answers will vary. Share the following information about reacting to conflict in these ways.

▲▲▲▲▲▲▲▲▲▲▲▲▲▲▲▲▲▲▲▲▲▲▲▲▲▲▲▲▲

Temporary withdrawal from a fight to gain control over angry feelings is often an appropriate technique. However, as a predominant method for handling conflict, withdrawal is costly. Consistent withdrawal indicates a giving up on the relationship and on self. ...

Over an extended period of time, a person who consistently withdraws from conflict in a relationship begins to turn away psychologically from that relationship.

People who insist on winning seem successful in life because they are achievers. But their relationships are usually superficial and often short-lived. ... Winning brings a sense of victory, but in the long run it may cost a person the relationship which means the most.

Yielding does bring outward peace, and the relationship can continue. However, a relationship in which one person does most of the yielding usually lacks a high level of mutual trust and intimacy. Giving and taking are in balance in a healthy relationship. In a one-sided relationship the giver will not feel very valuable to the taker, whose victories are at the giver's expense.

From *Merging Families* by Bobbie Reed, CPH, 1992, pp. 21–22.

▼▼▼▼▼▼▼▼▼▼▼▼▼▼▼▼▼▼▼▼▼▼▼▼▼

2. Allow participants to suggest possible ways Maria, Ross, and Jacob might have dealt more appropriately with the conflict.

Have a volunteer read aloud the situation about Jim and Betty.

3. Answers will vary.

4–5. Allow participants to suggest potential benefits of compromise. Then share the information that follows.

▲▲▲▲▲▲▲▲▲▲▲▲▲▲▲▲▲▲▲▲▲▲▲▲▲

In a compromise each person gives in a little so that the conflict is resolved without either person being the winner or loser. Each person wins a little and each loses a little. The fact that both parties are willing to compromise indicates that they consider their relationship to be more important than their differences. The payoff is a good relationship and acceptable resolutions to issues.

▼

Resolving a conflict acknowledges the importance of both the relationship and the issue without sacrificing either one. The solution belongs to both partners because they developed it together. And the joint investment of creative energy to resolve a problem brings increased intimacy to the relationship.

From *Merging Families* by Bobbie Reed, CPH, 1992, pp. 22–23.

▼▼▼▼▼▼▼▼▼▼▼▼▼▼▼▼▼▼▼▼▼▼▼▼▼▼▼

6. Allow one or two volunteers to share what they have written for each of these passages. Affirm the forgiveness, power, and strength Jesus offers to everyone, including those who desire to build strong marriages and healthy family relationships.

▲ Working it Through

Allow a minute or two for participants to work through this section individually, marking those things they are already doing and those they plan to do as they work to build a closer relationship with their spouses.

▲ To Do at Home

Encourage participants to do this activity during the week ahead.

▲ Closing Prayer

Lead or ask a volunteer to lead the group in a closing prayer, either praying the prayer printed in the Study Guide or praying extemporaneously.

Session 4

The Parenting Partnership

▲ Focus

Welcome everyone. Give each participant a copy of the Study Guide. Encourage participants to write their names on the front covers. Ask them to take the booklets home between sessions and to bring them back each time the group meets.

▲ Objectives

That by the power of the Holy Spirit working through God's Word the participants will

1. view their blended families the way God does—as gifts to one another, each in his or her particular role within the new family;

2. identify the obstacles in parenting a stepchild;

3. demonstrate a reliance upon God in Christ to make your blended family into one family sharing common joys and struggles, rather than two families living parallel lives.

▲ Opening Prayer

Begin the session with prayer, either praying extemporaneously or reading the prayer printed in the Study Guide.

▲ Focusing Our Attention

Say, **When biological parents from two families come together to form one family, the parenting issues**

must be dealt with in a loving and patient manner. While God views this new blending as one family, it takes time for the human participants to feel the same oneness. Ask participants to discuss their families in small groups of three or four.

▲ Becoming a Parent to Your Spouse's Children

Read or invite volunteers to read aloud the three paragraphs in this section. Then allow participants to work on the numbered items in pairs or small groups. After several minutes of sharing time, reassemble participants and invite comments from items one and two. Affirm the benefits God can bring those in blended families. Generally speaking, the more adults who love and care about a child, the better off he or she will be.

▲ Back to the Future

Allow several minutes for participants to respond privately to the items in this section. After allowing a brief amount of time for participants to think over these questions and to write their responses, move to the next section.

▲ Working as a Team

Read or have a volunteer read aloud this section. Then proceed immediately to the discussion items in the next section.

▲ For Discussion

Place participants into pairs or into small groups to discuss each of the items in this section. Then reassemble the whole group and invite comment about each item.

1. Participants may agree that God has no stepchildren in the sense that He regards those who love and trust in Him as His children. However, in another sense, we were brought

into His family were made heirs only by grace through faith in Christ Jesus. Biologically, Jesus Christ is the only Son of God.

2. Affirm comments that center around encouraging Bob to share his concern with Heather's mother and, rather than taking any direct action on his own, to rely on his wife to assume an active role in dealing with the situation.

▲ Help for Successful Parenting

Read through the suggestions as a whole group, pausing from time to time to allow members to comment. Invite additional suggestions and comments from the group.

▲ To Try at Home

Encourage participants to do this activity during the week ahead.

▲ Closing Prayer

Conclude the session either leading or inviting a volunteer to lead the group in prayer, praying extemporaneously or praying the prayer printed in the Study Guide.

Session 5

Helping Your Child Adjust

▲ Focus

Welcome everyone. Give each participant a copy of the
Study Guide. Encourage participants to write their names on
the front covers. Ask that they take the booklets home
between sessions and bring them back each time the group
meets.

▲ Objectives

That by the power of the Holy Spirit working through
God's Word participants will

1. demonstrate an increased understanding of how children struggle to adjust to life in a blended family and of the
God-given role of parents and stepparents in helping them
adjust;

2. identify the developmental issues influencing their
child's adjustment;

3. express reliance upon God to help them support their
children through physical and emotional changes.

▲ Opening Prayer

Invite participants to join you in praying the prayer
printed in the Study Guide. Or lead the group in prayer,
inviting group members to take part adding the thoughts and
petitions on their hearts. Conclude the prayer in Jesus' name.

▲ Focusing Our Attention

Read the introductory material. Comment that, by God's grace and with His blessing, stepparents can be "special-kind-of" parents for the children whose lives they touch in this unique role. Then ask participants to work in pairs or in small groups to do this activity.

▲ The Gift of Empathy

Read the first two paragraphs in this section to the group. Then have volunteers read the information provided in the Young Children, Ages 6–12, and Teenager categories aloud to the group. Pause between sections for comments and discussion. Begin each new age-level category with someone else reading. Ask participants to move into groups according to the age level of their children to respond to the questions in this section. Participants with children in more than one age grouping will need to make a choice. After several minutes of small-group sharing, reassemble the whole group. Invite general comments and insights before continuing with the next section.

▲ God's Help for Family Building

Work through this section as a whole group. Read the introductory paragraph aloud. As always, stress God's boundless love for us in Christ Jesus our Lord, the force that heals, motivates, and binds us to Himself and to one another. Continue by having participants read each of the passages aloud and by inviting applications for each from the group.

1. a. God promises to bless those who have committed themselves to Him. This promise can be especially meaningful as you face struggles in family life.

b. God invites those desiring wisdom to ask Him and He will provide it. God here indicates His ability and willingness to help parents and stepparents make wise parenting choices.

c. God brings many benefits to families as forgiveness and prayer are woven into the fabric of daily life.

▼

d. Families founded upon Jesus Christ are a community of faith. Christ promises a special blessing upon this fellowship. Affirm the value of family participation in family devotions and corporate worship.
2. Answers will vary.

▲ To Try at Home

Challenge participants to work through this section privately. Encourage them to set a goal to address one thing they would like to improve in their parenting.

▲ Closing Prayer

Conclude the session either leading or inviting a volunteer to lead the group in prayer, praying extemporaneously, or praying the prayer printed in the Study Guide.

Session 6

The Journey Forward

▲ Focus

Welcome everyone to the final session of this course. Make sure each participant has a copy of the Study Guide. Briefly review the topics covered in the preceding five sessions. Comment that today's session will wrap things up with a forward-looking emphasis on Christ-powered family building.

▲ Objectives

That by the power of the Holy Spirit working through God's Word the participants will

1. identify the building of a healthy blended family as a process in which Christ leads the way;

2. recognize the benefits of Christ's forgiveness, sacrifice, and healing for all families;

3. affirm the role of commitment, acceptance, and appreciation in blended family life with God's Word as the foundation;

4. build a sense of family unity by establishing traditions and goals, trusting in God's help and confident that with Him nothing is impossible.

▲ Opening Prayer

Invite participants to join you in praying the prayer printed in the Study Guide. Or lead the group in prayer, inviting group members to contribute the thoughts and petitions on their hearts. Conclude the prayer in Jesus' name.

▲ Focusing Our Attention

Invite participants to complete this activity with a partner, preferably someone other than a spouse. Reassemble everyone. Invite one or two brief comments about each item. Then continue with the next section.

▲ Coming Together

After reading through the introductory material in this section, invite participants to get into pairs or in small groups to work through the activity. Then reassemble and invite comments or responses for each item. Possible insights follow.

1. a.Christ Jesus is the only sure foundation upon which a family—or any institution or relationship—can be built.

b. The Spirit of God at work in those who by faith belong to God would have us approach life positively—looking for, focusing on, and celebrating the good things.

c. The power of the Gospel brings a desire to regard and act toward others as we, in turn, would have them regard and act toward us. Briefly refer to empathy as it was discussed in the previous session.

d. Knowing that the creator and all-powerful ruler of the entire universe has our personal best interests at heart can comfort and encourage parents and other family members in any and all circumstances.

e. All of us need the periodic reminder that God desires us to find our strength, hope, and direction in Him.

f. We can be encouraged, knowing that our God is capable of doing for us far beyond our ability to anticipate or even comprehend.

2. Responses will vary. Encourage participants to look for positive signs in their family life and to build on them.

▲ Acceptance and Appreciation

Work through this section as a whole group. Read the

information preceding item one aloud to the group. Then continue with the numbered items, reading the questions and soliciting responses from the group.

1. God hates sin. Nevertheless, He loved us even when we were held in the bondage of sin and lived as enemies of God, sending Jesus to pay our debt and earn forgiveness for us. Similarly, God's Spirit brings in believers the desire to love others unconditionally.
2. God desires His people to perform acts of love even when they don't feel inclined to do so.
3. Accept participants' responses.

▲ Commitment

Again, work together with the whole group to complete this section.

1. Affirm the order of commitment priorities this couple has adopted—God first, their marriage second, and thirdly their family. Point out that this order of priorities has the best interest of the family in mind.

2. Read the list aloud to the group. Ask participants to add ideas and suggestions of their own.

▲ Traditions

Read or paraphrase the introductory material to your group, underscoring the importance of establishing and continuing traditions and building positive family memories. Ask participants to review the list individually, checking those items they would like to begin in their families. After allowing ample time for everyone to read the items and respond, invite additional ideas and suggestions from the group.

▲ To Try at Home

Encourage participants to do this activity and others from the previous section.

▲ Closing Prayer

Thank everyone for taking part in this and all other sessions. Conclude the course, using the prayer printed in the Study Guide.

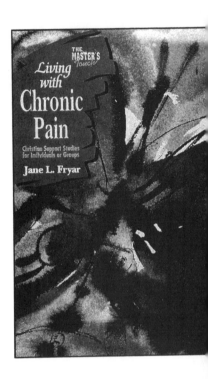